The Easy to Make Paper Airplane Book

Created for kids by a kid

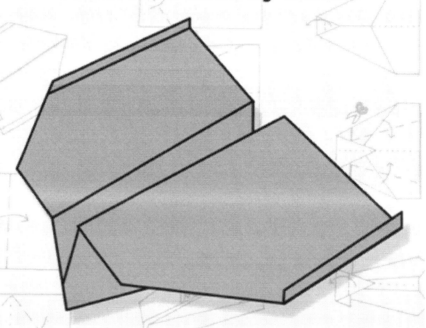

16 great airplane designs made from common notebook paper and ready to fly

created by Lane Simpson

The Easy to Make Paper Airplane Book

by Lane Simpson

Created for kids by a kid

This book teaches you to make paper airplanes the old-fashioned way. Each airplane uses regular notebook paper, so there is no special paper to buy. Most of the designs were discovered and created by Lane Simpson when he was 10 years old, and they have been successfully used by children of all ages. Your kids will make flying airplanes right away.

Easy to follow directions and illustrations make this a great book for practice in following directions, coordination, understanding flight surfaces, and design. Discussions on the basics of flight are included.

The Easy to Make Paper Airplane Book

Created for kids by a kid

Created by Lane Simpson

Table of Contents

HOW THE PLANE STAYS IN THE AIR

LIFT: Airplanes need a force to keep them in the air. They get this force when air moves over the flight surfaces (wings) and provide lift. Lift is a force upward on top of the wing. Low air pressure is created when the air going over the top of a wing must travel faster than the air below the wing. The side view of a real airplane wing is:

Lower Pressure

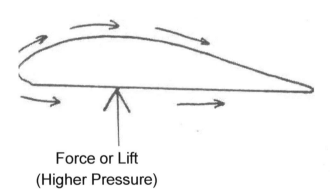

Force or Lift
(Higher Pressure)

Paper airplane wings usually don't have as much lift as real airplanes because the paper is thin and cannot hold its shape well. Nevertheless, paper airplanes do achieve lift and some can fly long distances (try Dad's Favorite in this book).

CONTROL SURFACES

Elevator - This control surface is located at the rear of the airplane.

When elevators (or elevons when they are combined with ailerons) are turned up, the tail of the plane is forced down and the nose up. When turned down, elevators force the tail up and the nose down. This action controls the "pitch" of the airplane. Pitch determines the angle of ascent (Upward Travel) or descent (Downward Travel) of the plane, that is, whether it is going up or down.

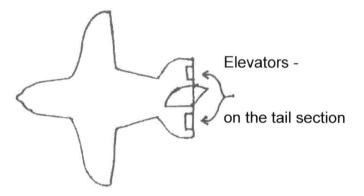

Elevators - on the tail section

Rudder - This surface is vertical and to the rear of the plane in almost all planes. On many paper airplanes, the rudder controls are usually made on the outside edge of each wing rather than on a single stalk in the center rear of the plan.

So, most paper airplanes don't have a tail where the rudder would normally be. So, most paper airplanes don't have a tail where the rudder would normally be. The rudder controls "yaw" or left/right movement of the nose. The rudder helps the plane make left and right turns.

Rudder-

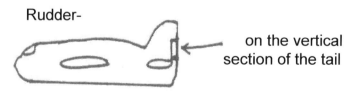

on the vertical section of the tail

Aileron - These surfaces are on the wing's trailing edge (opposite the edge of the wings that first cuts through the air). On large airplanes, they operate together but in opposite directions, to make the plane bank left or right. This banking is called "roll" and it happens when lift is applied to the top of one wing and the bottom of the other wing at the same time. On most paper airplanes, the ailerons are combined with elevators on the trailing edge of the large wing. These are called "elevons."

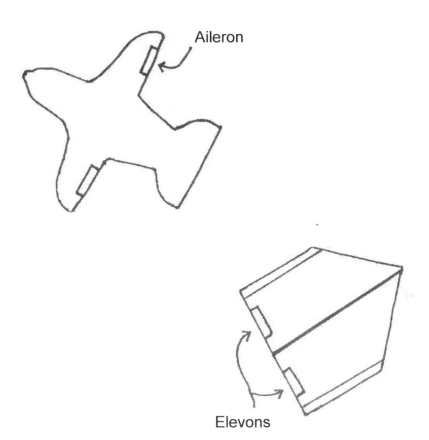

Aileron

Elevons

IF YOUR PLANE NOSE DIVES

This problem is brought about when there is not enough lift toward the front of the plane and/or too much lift on the tail. To correct this problem, fold the elevators (or elevons) on the back of the plane upward slightly and fly it. If the nose continues downward in flight, raise the elevators more, until the plane flies level. Experiment and try new ideas frequently. You can have fun, learn more, and you can always make a new plane.

IF YOUR PLANE STALLS NOSE-UP

This problem is caused by poor lift in the back of the plane. To correct this problem, fold the elevators (elevons) down (see page 7) and fly the plane. Make adjustments until you achieve level flight (see also **If Your Plane Nose Dives**). If your plane design does not have elevators (elevons), make them (see page 7).

IF YOU WANT YOUR PLANE TO TURN RIGHT OR LEFT

To make your plane bank into a left or right turn, first refer to page 7 regarding the effects of ailerons. Ailerons are control surfaces on the wings that allow banking by increasing or decreasing lift on each side of the airplane. In real airplanes, when the left aileron moves up slightly, the right aileron moves slightly down. If the right aileron moves up strongly, the left moves down strongly.

On paper airplanes you can raise or lower one at a time or both in opposite directions at the same time in order to bank the plane.

To make your plane bank left, raise a part of the trailing edge (back edge) of the left wing. Make the aileron about 1/2" to 1" across. Next, lower a part of the trailing edge of the right wing slightly. Make adjustments in order to determine the degree or steepness of the banking.

To make your plane bank right, first reverse the process, with the right aileron pushed upward and the left aileron pushed downward. Banking a plane makes it roll. Use your knowledge of control surfaces to control your plane the way you want.

Roll Axis (Ailerons)

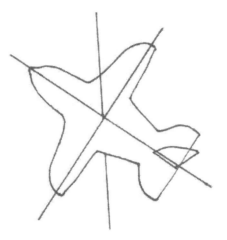

Pitch Axis (Elevons)

Yaw Axis (Rudder)

Dihedral is the slight upward tilt of the wings from the body of the airplane. This produces a slight V-shape to the wings when viewed from the front of the plane. Dihedral gives stability to your planes, which is very important. Most designs in this book tend to open in the middle of the plane, causing the wings to naturally droop down a little. You will need to bend the wings up in order to counter this droop. Looking from the front, your planes should usually look like this:

Straight
(viewing plane from the front)

Angled up in the middle
(viewing plane from the front)

Special Note to Parents

If your child becomes interested in paper airplanes, you may well end up with airplanes all over the house and an unquenchable desire for paper in your child.

Here are a few suggestions:

1.   Buy copy paper by the ream - about $8.00 per ream. It is good for drawing as well. Or, use regular notebook paper.

2.   Other sources of airplane materials:

   a)   backing paper for stickers
   b)   perforated cards found in magazines
   c)   old letters and school papers
   d)   used paper from mom or dad's office

3. Designate a plastic basket or paper grocery bag for the "keepers" - all other planes are thrown away or recycled. If your child begins designing their own planes, enjoy that they are learning and using their imagination. Think of throwaways as lessons learned.

How to Make the Airplanes

1.   Use the suggested paper.

2.   Keep the paper flat on the table when you work.

3.   Do not turn the plane over unless the directions tell you to do so.

4.   Read the directions carefully, look at the diagram, and then follow the directions.

5.   If the plane does not fly well on the first try, crease the folds again and be sure all sides line up. Creases should be made by applying pressure to the fold with your thumbnail or hard object.

         Read the section on flight surfaces if your plane continues to fly poorly. Maybe all you need is to tweak (make fine adjustments to) the elevons. Keep experimenting and you will get it right. Use your imagination.

6.   Safety Tips: Throw your airplanes in a safe place where they will not hit anyone. When you are outside, be sure you are in a safe place that is not near a street or moving cars. Be careful never to run into the street after your airplane. Do not throw your airplane at another person or animal, and remember, airplanes can change directions quickly and do not always fly in a straight line.

Glossary of Words and Symbols

_____ Shows the sides of the paper.

-- -- -- -- -- -- -- -- -- -- -- -- -- Shows where the fold is to be made.

· · · · · · · · · · · · · · · · · · · Shows a crease made from a previous fold.

-- -- -- -- --> Shows the direction the fold is to be made.

a, b, c, d, X's Letters are used to help in the direction.

Long way Fold to make the center fold down the longest part of the paper.

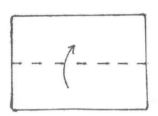

13

Short way

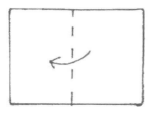

Fold to make the center fold down the shortest part of the paper.

Thumb crease - To fold paper over with your thumb. The fold is the size of your thumb and used on the back of wings.

Notebook paper - Standard 3-hole notebook paper or plain copy paper.

3 TAIL FLYER

Type of paper to use: **Notebook paper**

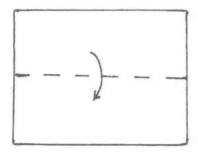

Fold paper long way. Open paper.

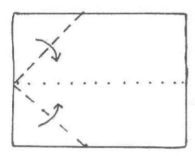

Fold corners to meet at centerfold line.

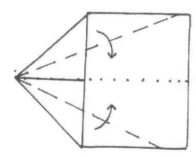

Fold new corners to meet at center crease.

3 TAIL FLYER - 2

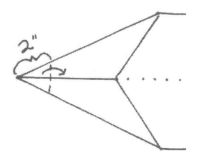

Fold point back - line up on centerfold

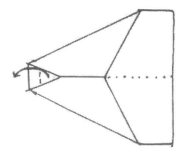

Fold tip back over the fold you just made. Be sure the end of the tip goes past the airplane body.

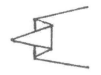

The tip should look like this:

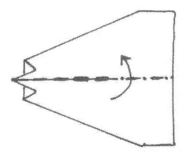

Fold airplane in half at center crease.

Fold top down to form a wing.

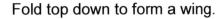

Turn the plane over and do the same thing on that side.

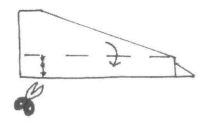

Cut through the two layers of paper that form the plane body - cut up to the fold that begins the wings.

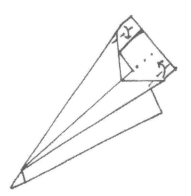

Push the cut section of the plane straight up to make a fin. Push the wings together, press on the bottom of the fin and top of the fin to keep it straight up. Tape underneath if needed. Fold the tips of the wings up, press on the fold and let go.

Flying Instructions:

Hold in middle of the plane body (fuselage) with your thumb and four fingers. Keep the nose of the plane up just a little bit and throw it as you would throw a baseball or a rock into a lake.

THE HIGH FLYER

Type of paper to use: **Construction paper**

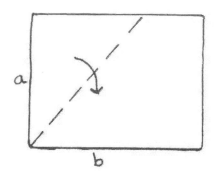

Use long way fold. Fold the corner of paper over - line up side **a** with side **b**. Push down on fold. Open paper.

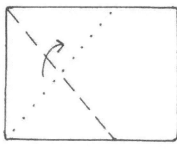

Repeat on the other side. Open it up and turn paper over.

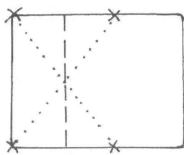

Fold the top of the paper down - match at the **X**'s. Press on fold.

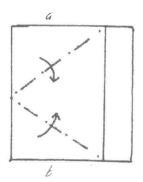

Fold over each corner at the fold lines. Sides **a** and **b** should meet in the middle.

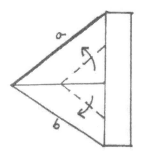

Fold the points of the top layer up to meet sides **a** and **b**. Press on fold.

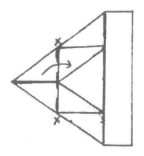

Fold the point of the plane down - fold line should be at the **X**'s.

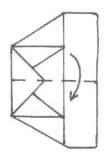 Fold in half.

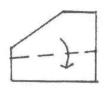 Fold each side down to form wings.

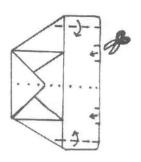 Fold the sides of the wings up. Make small cuts at the end of the wings and fold these up (elevons).

<u>Flying Instruction:</u>

Hold in front part of fuselage - throw upward

BUZZARD

This plane reminds me of a buzzard with large outstretched wings, soaring slowly and riding the hot "thermals" – rising air currents - to stay aloft.

It's good on calm days or indoors.

Type of paper to use: Copy paper

Turn paper long way.

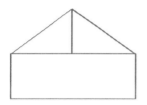

Fold each side to the midline, leaving about 3 inches of paper at the bottom. Crease well.

Fold the nose down and crease.

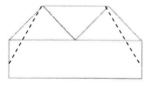

Fold the outside wing edges in and crease along dotted fold lines.

BUZZARD - 2

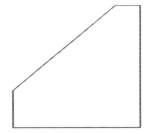

Fold the right side onto the left side and crease so that the edges of the wings line up.

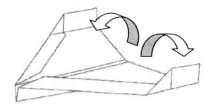

Fold the wings down along the fold.

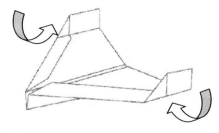

Fold the winglets up.

The wings will have a slight "V" shape when viewed from the front. Add elevators along the back edge of the wings if necessary.

Flying Instruction:

Hold in middle of fuselage. Holding the plane up a little bit, throw it gently.

STAR CRUISER

Type of paper to use: **Notebook paper**

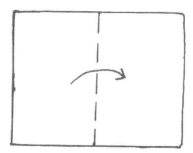

Fold paper in half, short way.
Open paper.

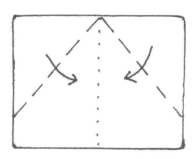

Fold corners to meet at the
middle fold.

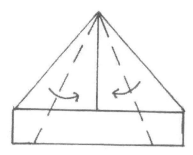

Fold sides over again to meet at
middle fold (will overlap at
bottom).

STAR CRUISER - 2

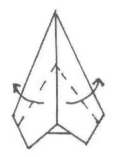

Fold wings back at dotted lines - wings overlap body at each side.

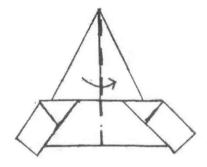

Fold plane in half - line up wings - crease the fold.

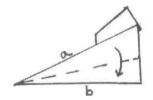

Fold down the wing on the dotted line. Match side **a** with side **b** on both sides.

Fold wing sides up.

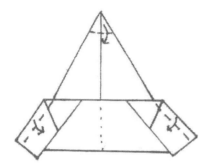

Fold nose of plane back into centerfold. Press sides together at tip to hold it in place.

Flying Instruction:

Hold in middle of fuselage. Holding the plane up a little bit, throw it gently.

SPINNING HELICOPTER

Type of paper to use: Notebook paper

Okay, it's not really a plane but
It is a flying craft. It flies down only.

The helicopter is a classic design that
spins rapidly as it descends. It works
great when dropped from a high place.

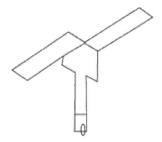

Try different amounts of weight on the
bottom tab.
Notice that the helicopter spins in different
directions depending on which direction the
rotors are folded.

You can make 6 helicopters by cutting on the dotted lines. Make 6
sets of dotted lines spaced the same.

Take one of the pieces and cut in
the middle one-third the length as
shown.

Next, cut on the dotted lines.
Do not cut all the way across,
just part way on either side then
down the length.

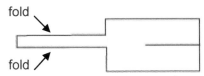

fold

fold

Fold each side at the fold lines.
One will overlap the other.

SPINNING HELICOPTER

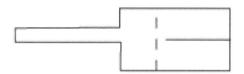

Fold the end upwards toward the rotors.

Fold rotors down in opposite directions. Attach a paper clip to the bottom tab. Drop from the helicopter from high above your head and watch it spin as it falls slowly.

Experiment with different weights (2 paper clips, a blob of gum – outside only!)

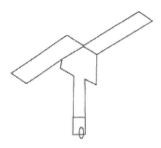

Also, fold rotors in opposite direction from your first helicopter. Does it spin the same direction? You can change the angle on the rotors to see how it affects flight.

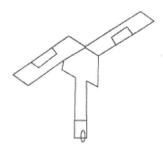

You can even put little elevators on each rotor, and see what it does when they are "up," or "down," or even "one up one down" elevators."

Flying Instruction:

Hold in middle of fuselage. Holding the plane up a little bit, throw it gently.

DAD'S FAVORITE

Type of paper to use: **Notebook paper**

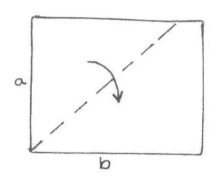

Use short way fold. Fold the corner of paper and line up side **a** and **b**. Open paper.

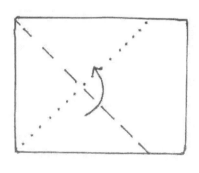

Repeat on the other side. Open paper.

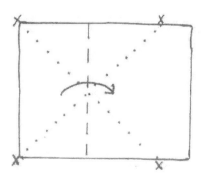

Fold top of paper down - match
X's

DAD'S FAVORITE - 2

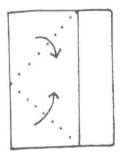

Fold each corner at crease to meet in the middle.

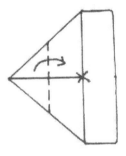

Fold point down to touch **X**.

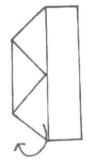

Turn the plane over.

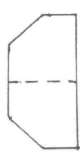

Fold plane in half.

Fold down each wing - crease angles up a little in back.

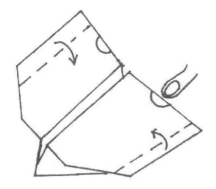

Fold edges of wings up.

Thumb crease the back of the wings, creating small elevons.

Flying Instruction:

Hold in front part of the fuselage and give it a strong throw upward. Great for flying outdoors and in wide-open places.

THE BI-WING GLIDER

Type of paper to use: legal size paper or notebook paper

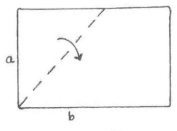

Fold short way. Fold corner of paper - line up side **a** with side **b**. Open paper.

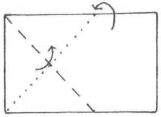

Repeat on other side. Open paper and turn the paper over.

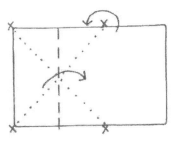

Fold top part of paper down to meet **X**'s - Open. Turn the whole sheet over again.

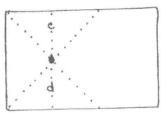

Push the middle dot area in. Bring creased lines (**c** and **d**) together in middle of paper. Push top triangle down to cover the fold in lines **c** and **d**.

THE BI-WING GLIDER- 2

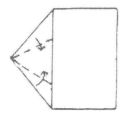

Using the top layer only, fold each corner of the triangle where sides meet in the middle.

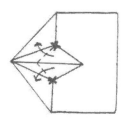

Fold points back up. Be sure fold begins at corner **X**'s.

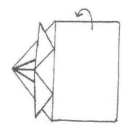

Turn it over.

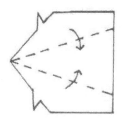

Fold sides to meet in the middle.

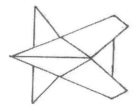

Turn it over.

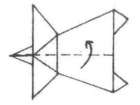

Fold in half.

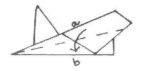

On both sides, fold top layer to form a wing. Match side **a** with side **b**. Repeat on the other side

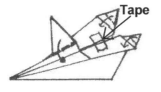

Fold the top wings down to form the bi-wing. Thumb crease the back points of the main wings. Tape the fuselage behind the top wing.

Flying Instruction:

Hold in the middle of the plane. Throw hard, like a baseball.
If needed, fold top wing up (see top wing diagram).

FLYING RING

Type of paper to use: Notebook paper

Sometimes things fly when they don't look like an airplane. This flying ring is one of those things

Tell your friends you can make a circle fly, and let them laugh until you throw this circle then watch them be amazed.

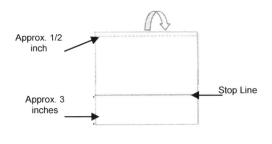

Approx. 1/2 inch

Approx. 3 inches

Stop Line

Fold along the first dotted line.
It should be about a half inch wide.
Continue folding the strip over itself until you reach the stop line.
Make firm creases with each fold.

Approx. 7 folds

Stop Line

Your paper should look like this when you reach the stop line, approximately three inches from the bottom.

Grab both ends of the paper and pull it back and forth over the edge of the table to make the paper start to curl with the folded edge on the outside. Shape it into a cylinder and overlap the edges by ½ inch. Tape the outside seam to hold it. Now get your friends to see your odd plane fly!

Flying Instruction:

Throw the flying ring with the folded edge forward by letting it roll off your fingertips, spinning it as you release.

THE SWOOPER

Type of paper to use: Notebook paper

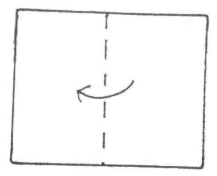

Short fold the paper in half.

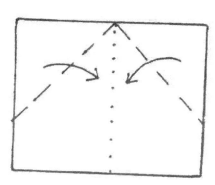

Fold corners to meet at the center line. Turn it over.

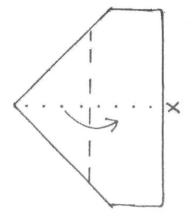

Fold the tip of the paper to meet at the **x**.

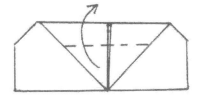

Fold the tip of the plane back over - it will overlap by 1" to 1 1/2".

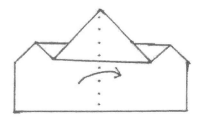

Turn it over. Fold in half at crease line.

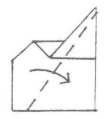

Fold the wings down on both sides.

Flying Instruction:

Throw high in the air and hard. You need plenty of space as it banks to the left. Try experimenting with flight surface changes.

THE FLOATING FROG

Type of paper to use: **Notebook paper**

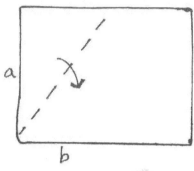

Fold short way. Fold corner of paper over. Line up side **a** with side **b**. Push down on fold. Open paper.

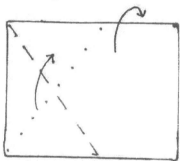

Repeat on the other side. Open it up and turn the paper over.

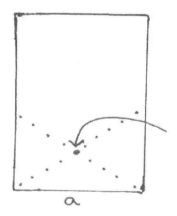

Rotate the paper so side **a** is facing you. Push the center of the fold down with your index finger.

FLOATING FROG – 2

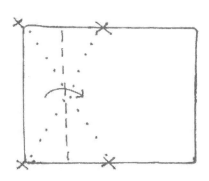

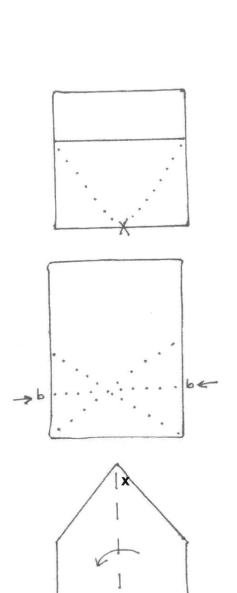

Fold the paper up. Match at the **X**'s. Press on the fold.

Pick up the paper, open it, and underneath the paper push at point where all the folds meet - at **X**.

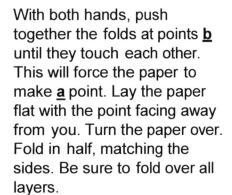

With both hands, push together the folds at points **b** until they touch each other. This will force the paper to make **a** point. Lay the paper flat with the point facing away from you. Turn the paper over. Fold in half, matching the sides. Be sure to fold over all layers.

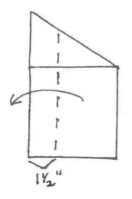

Fold the top half over the center of the plane to form a wing. The center section should be 1 ½ inches deep. Turn over and repeat on the other side.

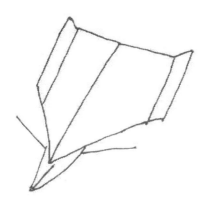

Hold plane and open wings out. The small wings under the top one are used to make the frog legs.

Using the small wings only, fold down at the 1/3 mark of the wing, then up at the 2/3 mark. Repeat on the other side.

FLOATING FROG - 4

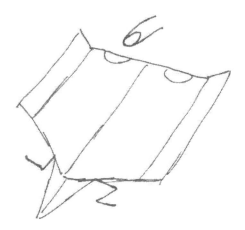

On the top wing, fold up the sides. Thumb crease the back of the wings, to create elevons.

Flying Instructions:

Hold the plane in the middle and throw straight up in the air. The frog will gently hop to the ground.

SPACE PLANE FLYER

Type of paper to use: Notebook or copy paper

This plane starts out like the Dart but has an extra set of folds on the wings. Be sure your creases are sharp and firm.

This plane will really "take off" flying fast, far, and probably rolling as it goes. Try elevon changes.

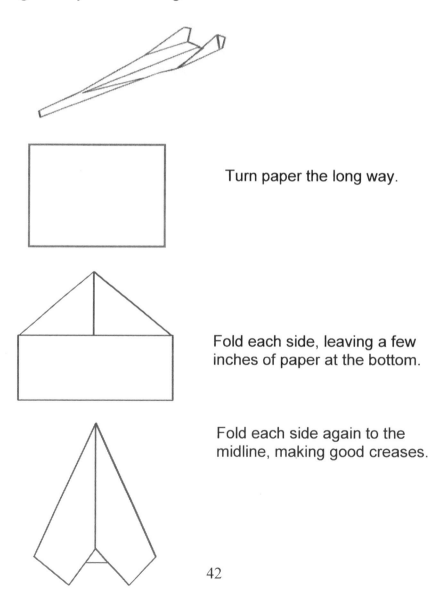

Turn paper the long way.

Fold each side, leaving a few inches of paper at the bottom.

Fold each side again to the midline, making good creases.

42

SPACE PLANE FLYER – LONG FLYER - 2

Fold each side again to the midline. Creases should be firm. Press hard with your thumbnail, a coin, or other hard object.

Fold the nose down toward the midline.

Fold the plane at the midline so the sides match up.

Open the plane, making small vertical winglets at the tip of each wing.

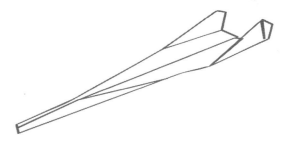

Flying Instructions:

Hold in middle of the plane body (fuselage) with your thumb and four fingers. Keep the nose of the plane up just a little bit and throw it as you would throw a baseball or a rock into a lake.

THE GLIDING JET

Type of paper to use: **Notebook paper**

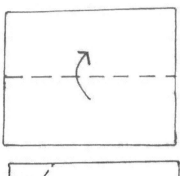

Fold in half long way. Open up.

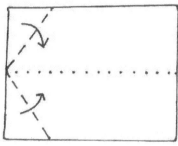

Fold corner ends to meet in the middle.

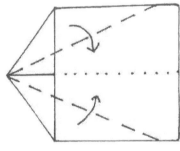

Fold new corners to meet in the middle.

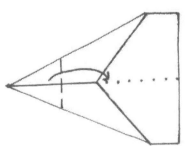

Fold point back over plane - point extends just past end of other folds.

THE GLIDING JET - 2

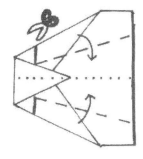

Cut through the plane body
about 1 inch from front, cut
from the edge to the over-
lapping triangle. Fold the sides
over from the cut.

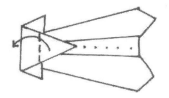

Fold point back - point will
over- lap plane body.

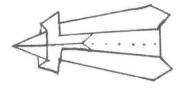

Fold plane in half.

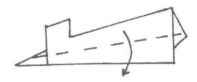

Fold both sides down to form
wings.

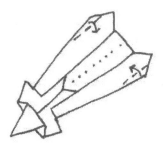

Fold sides of wings up.

Flying Instruction:

Hold up - throw hard for jet, throw gently for glider.

THE SOARING EAGLE

Type of paper to use: **Legal size paper or notebook paper**

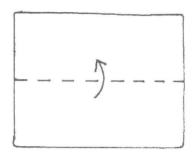

Fold in half long way.

Open up.

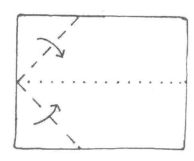

Fold corners to meet in the middle.

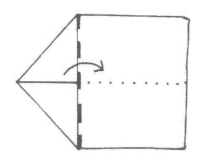

Fold triangle point down.

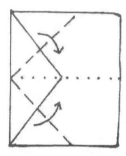

Fold new corners to meet in the middle of the paper.

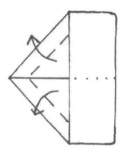

Fold top points back over the triangle (point will overlap plane).

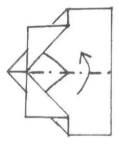

Fold in half.

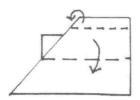

Fold half the plane down to form a wing. Do the same on the other wing sides.

Flying Instructions:

Throw high and lightly. Remember, keep experimenting with throws, elevons, and dihedral. Try things your imagination tells you to do.

X BIRD

Type of paper to use: Notebook or copy paper

This unusual plane gets its name from its two sets of nearly symmetrical wings that resemble an "X" when viewed from the top. This plane is very aerobatic, and will tend to loop if thrown hard outdoors.

stop line

Fold along the first fold line.
Continue folding this strip over itself until you reach the stop line. The stop line will be just short of the middle of the paper. Make firm creases with each fold.
5-6 folds, approximately ¾ inch wide, are needed.

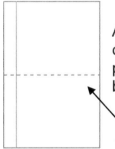

After you reach the stop line, flip your paper over and fold it in half. The two flat sides of the paper should touch and the thick folds should be on top and opposite the two flat sides.

fold lines

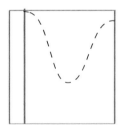

Thick folded
part on top

Cut along the cut lines while keeping the paper folded tightly together so both wings match.

Do not cut thick folded part. Cut next to it and follow the cut lines.

X BIRD - 2

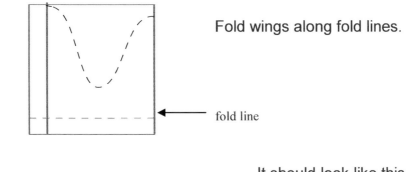

Fold wings along fold lines.

fold line

It should look like this.

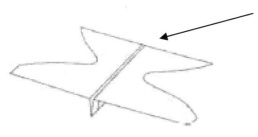

Fold the front winglets up and the back winglets down.

Front winglets
folded up

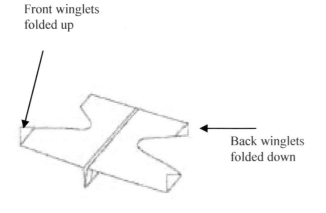

Back winglets
folded down

The wings will have a "V" shape when viewed from the front.

Flying Instruction:

Hold in middle of fuselage. Holding the plane up a little bit, throw it gently.

PETE'S PLANE

Type of paper to use: **Notebook paper**

Not all birds can fly, but many of them want to fly. Pete the Penguin loves flying, but he needs you to make him an airplane.

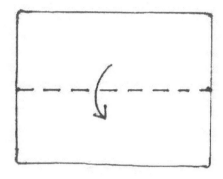

Fold in half long way. Open up.

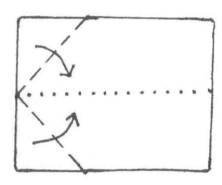

Fold corners to meet in the middle.

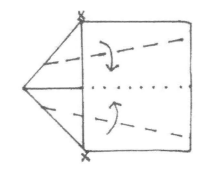

Fold sides in at an angle. The **X**'s will meet in the middle.

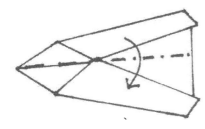

Fold plane in half.

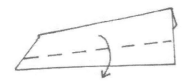

Fold wings down on both sides.

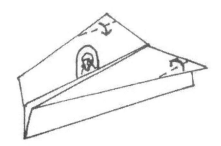

Fold sides of wings at the end. Trace Pete (or photocopy and cut), taping him in the cockpit.

Flying Instruction:

Hold in middle of fuselage. Holding the plane up a little bit, throw it gently.

Pete

DART – STEALTH FIGHTER - 1

Type of paper to use: Notebook or copy paper

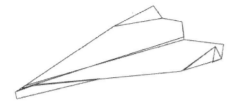

A fast flyer, this airplane has a nice tail design, it folds easily, and is responsive to elevon changes. It is easy to fold and an all around great flier.

Add some up elevon if necessary to produce stable flight.

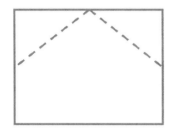

Turn paper sideways or long way.

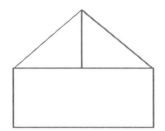

Fold each side, leaving a few inches of paper at the bottom.

Fold each side again, to the midline, making good creases.

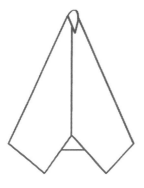

Fold the nose down toward the midline.

Fold the plane at the midline so the two sides match up.

Open the plane, making small vertical winglets at the tip of each wing.

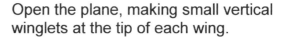

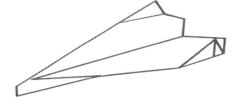

Experiment with the wings pushed up or down in the center.

Flying Instructions:

Hold in middle of the plane body (fuselage) with your thumb and four fingers. Keep the nose of the plane up just a little bit and throw it as you would throw a baseball or a rock into a lake.

Flying High with Your Imagination

The Easy to Make Paper Airplane Book
By Lane Simpson

Your children's fun will take off while they learn the basics of flight from this easy to use book. All designs have step by step instructions and are tested by children all over the world. All your child needs is notebook paper and off they go.

Make up your own characters like Pete. Draw them, color them, and cut them out. Color your planes, too. Name your characters and give them a personality.

Create your own adventures with your characters and planes.

Tell a story about them or write your stories on paper. Share them with your friends. Where will your characters fly? What would they do? Will your planes do any special tricks?

Be creative and make up your own kinds of flying objects, too. What would you call your planes? What's special about them?

Keep track of your planes and characters. Make your own book about paper airplanes.

Paper airplanes have made my imagination soar. I hope it does the same for you.

Lane

To contact Lane with any helpful suggestions for the book, go to www.drdalecoach.com, or mail to: Lane Simpson, P.O. Box 2054, Venice, FL 34284.

The Easy to Make Paper Airplane Book is available for Kindle and Nook. Look for it on Amazon or Barnes and Noble.

Lane is interested in any new designs you make that you want to share with him. Maybe your design will get into the next book!

ISBN 978-1501083716

62523502R00035

Made in the USA
Lexington, KY
10 April 2017